ABDO
Publishing Company

SKELETAL
System

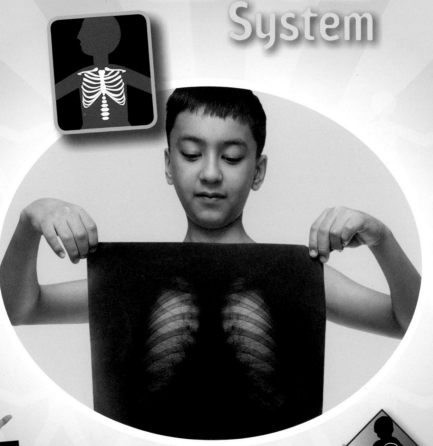

BODY SYSTEMS

Buddy BOOKS
Body Systems

A Buddy Book by **Sarah Tieck**

VISIT US AT
www.abdopublishing.com

Published by ABDO Publishing Company, 8000 West 78th Street, Edina, Minnesota 55439.

Copyright © 2011 by Abdo Consulting Group, Inc. International copyrights reserved in all countries. No part of this book may be reproduced in any form without written permission from the publisher. Buddy Books™ is a trademark and logo of ABDO Publishing Company.

Printed in the United States of America, North Mankato, Minnesota.
092010
012011

 PRINTED ON RECYCLED PAPER

Coordinating Series Editor: Rochelle Baltzer
Contributing Editors: Megan M. Gunderson, BreAnn Rumsch, Marcia Zappa
Graphic Design: Jenny Christensen
Cover Photograph: *iStockphoto*: ©iStockphoto.com/Mik122.
Interior Photographs/Illustrations: *Eighth Street Studio* (pp. 5, 22); *Getty Images*: Peter Cade (p. 29); *iStockphoto*: ©iStockphoto.com/fatihhoca (p. 30), ©iStockphoto.com/hartcreations (p. 15), ©iStockphoto.com/jgroup (p. 17), ©iStockphoto.com/MorePixels (p. 15), ©iStockphoto.com/mpabild (pp. 7, 23), ©iStockphoto.com/Raycat (p. 11), ©iStockphoto.com/red_frog (p. 9); *Peter Arnold, Inc.*: Marth Copper (p. 22), Ed Reschke (p. 19); *Photo Researchers, Inc.*: BSIP (p. 21); *Shutterstock*: Blamb (p. 15), Hank Frentz (p. 17), hkannn (p. 23), Sebastian Kaulitzki (pp. 11, 13), Douglas Litchfield (p. 13), michaeljung (p. 27), Paul Matthew Photography (p. 25), skyhawk (p. 17), Suzanne Tucker (p. 30).

Library of Congress Cataloging-in-Publication Data

Tieck, Sarah, 1976-
  Skeletal system / Sarah Tieck.
    p. cm. -- (Body systems)
  ISBN 978-1-61613-502-7
  1. Human skeleton--Juvenile literature. 2. Bones--Juvenile literature. I. Title.
  QM101.T54 2011
  612.7'5--dc22
                          2010019651

Table of Contents

Amazing Body

Your body is amazing! It does thousands of things each day. Your body parts help you grow, walk, and stand.

Groups of body parts make up body systems. Each system does important work. The skeletal system helps support and move your body. Let's learn more about it!

Your skeletal system is located all over your body.

Working Together

Your skeletal system is inside your body. You can feel it through your skin. It is made up of your body's skeleton. This includes your bones and the **tissues** that cushion and connect them.

Your skeleton helps give your body shape. Its size establishes how tall you are. And, your skeleton **protects** your inner **organs**.

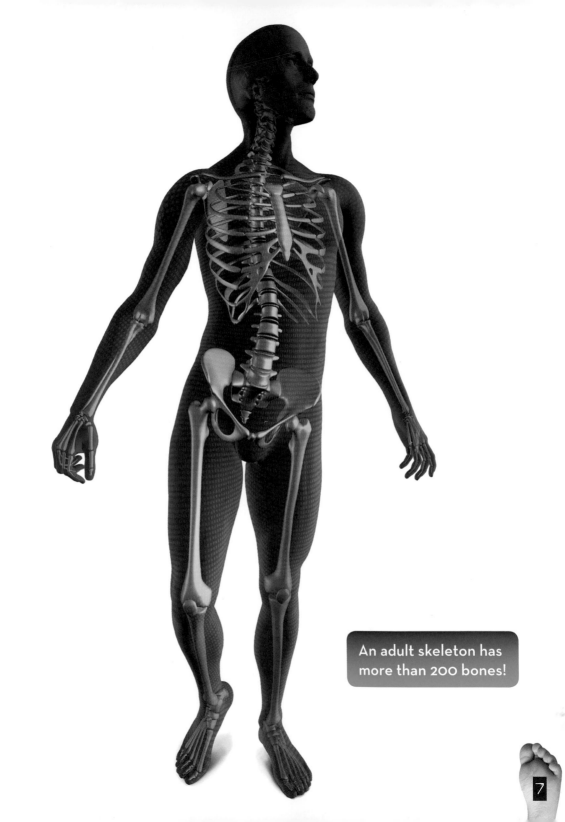

An adult skeleton has more than 200 bones!

Bare Bones

The bones in your skeleton come in many different shapes. They are made to fit in certain parts of your body.

Your skeleton's main parts include the skull, the spine, and the ribs. Each of these has a special job to do.

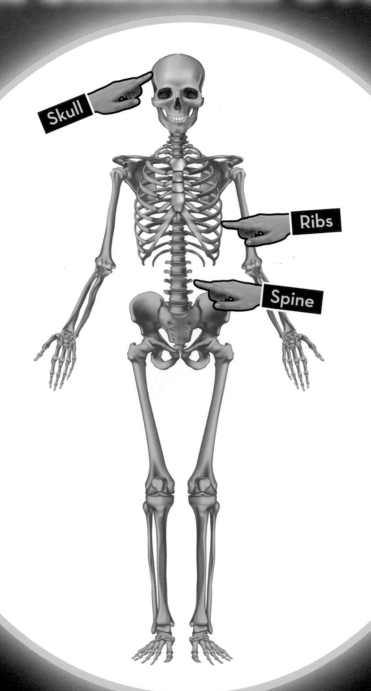

Press on the top of your head. The hard bone you feel is your skull. It includes 22 bones. They **protect** your brain and shape your face.

Your spine starts at the back of your neck. It reaches down the center of your back. It is made of many small bones called vertebrae. They circle and protect your **spinal cord**.

Inside your torso, you normally have 24 ribs. They protect your heart and lungs. Your top 14 ribs connect to a bone in your chest. It is called the breastbone, or sternum.

How It Sounds

vertebrae (VUHR-tuh-bray)
sternum (STUHR-nuhm)

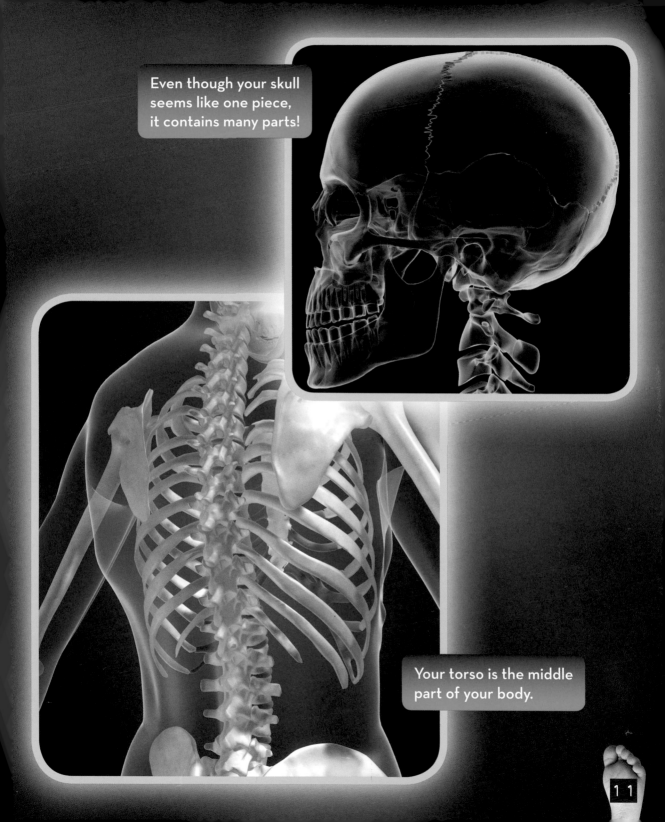

Even though your skull seems like one piece, it contains many parts!

Your torso is the middle part of your body.

Out on a Limb

Arms and legs, or limbs, help you move. Each arm has three main bones. Just one wrist and hand has 27 bones! All those little bones let you move your hands and pick up objects.

There are three main bones in each of your legs. Each ankle and foot has 26 bones! They help you run and walk.

How It Sounds

limb (LIHM)

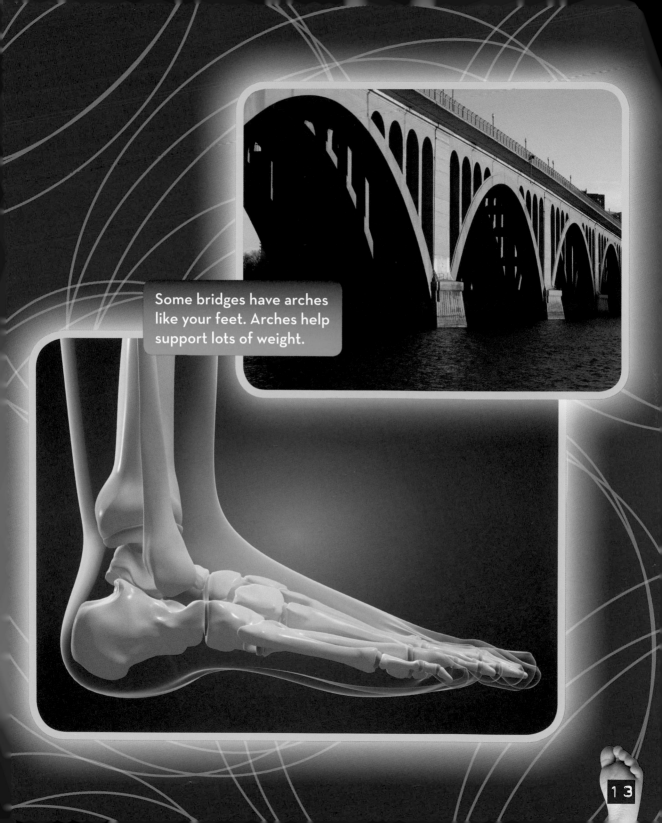

Some bridges have arches like your feet. Arches help support lots of weight.

Support System

Bones alone won't let you walk and run. They work with ligaments, tendons, and **muscles** to help you move.

Ligaments hold bones together. Tendons connect muscles to bones. And, muscles provide power to move bones.

Your skeleton also has strong, **flexible tissue** called cartilage. It pads the ends of your bones. And, it gives your body shape where there are no bones.

How It Sounds

ligament (LIH-guh-muhnt)
cartilage (KAHR-tuh-lihj)

14

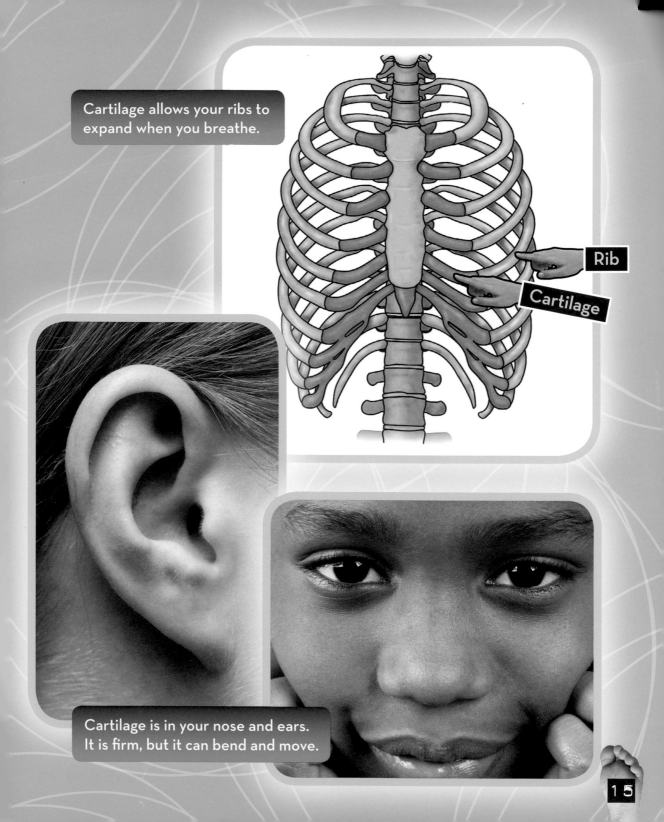

Cartilage allows your ribs to expand when you breathe.

Rib

Cartilage

Cartilage is in your nose and ears. It is firm, but it can bend and move.

Ligaments, tendons, **muscles**, and cartilage are important to your joints. Joints are places on your skeleton where two or more bones meet.

Some joints allow your body to move. These include ball-and-socket joints, pivot joints, and hinge joints. Other joints are fixed, which means they don't move. Fixed joints connect most of your skull bones.

Your hip is a ball-and-socket joint. It allows your leg to move.

At the top of your spine is a pivot joint. It allows you to turn your head.

Your elbow is a hinge joint. It allows your arm to bend.

The enamel coating on your teeth is the hardest tissue in your body. It is harder than bone!

No Bones About It

Your bones are living parts of your body. Blood is made in bones. Also, bones store **minerals** that keep your body healthy and strong.

Because bones are alive, they are always changing. They break down and build up.

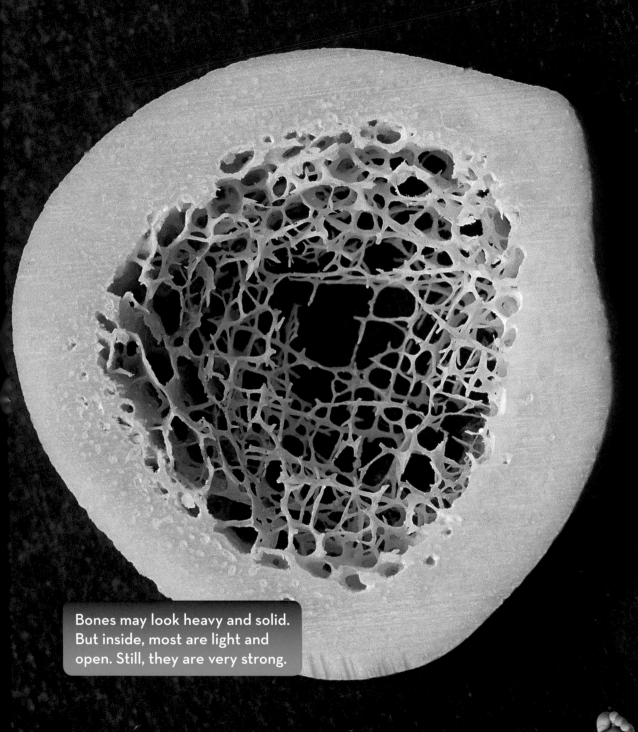

Bones may look heavy and solid.
But inside, most are light and
open. Still, they are very strong.

Bones have layers. On the outside is hard **tissue** called compact bone. Beneath that is spongy bone. Long tubes called **blood vessels** run through the layers.

Deep inside many bones is bone marrow. There are two types of this jellylike tissue. Red bone marrow makes new blood cells for your whole body. Yellow bone marrow stores fat.

INSIDE YOUR BONES

Spongy Bone

Compact Bone

Red Bone Marrow

Yellow Bone Marrow

Brain Food

Why do scientists look for old bones?

They learn about human history by studying bones. Sometimes, bones tell scientists about a person's health, lifestyle, or appearance. Scientists can often tell if the bones belonged to a man or a woman!

What parts of your body have the most bones?

Your hands and feet have the most bones. This is why they can move and bend in so many directions.

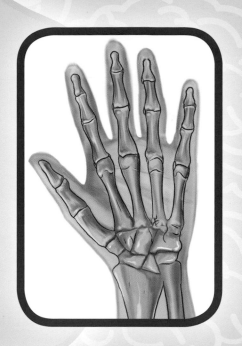

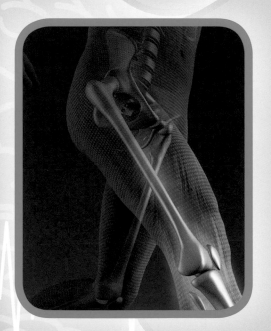

What are your longest bones?

Your femurs, or upper leg bones, are your longest bones. They support your weight when you walk, jump, run, and stand!

Knock Knock

Activities and accidents can harm your skeletal system. Your bones can break or crack. And if you tear your tendons or ligaments, your bones may not move correctly. Illnesses can also harm your bones.

Age affects bones, too. As people grow old, their bones may become weak. And, their cartilage may wear down.

A broken bone can heal itself. A doctor usually puts a cast around it. This helps it heal correctly.

You can do things to avoid harming your skeletal system. Make sure you get enough calcium in your diet. This **mineral** keeps bones healthy and strong. And, wear the right gear to **protect** yourself when you play sports.

Some people may need to see a doctor about their bones. Doctors have tools to see bones inside the body. They can also test inside the bones.

Doctors take X-rays to see bones. This helps them know if a bone has been hurt.

An Important System

Think about how important your bones are. Without them, you would be a big pile of mushy **organs**! By learning about your skeletal system, you can **protect** it. Then, you can make good choices to keep your body healthy!

It is important to take good care of your bones while you are young. Most people's bones stop growing in their 20s.

WORK IT OUT

✔ Exercise strengthens your bones. So, get your friends together for a game of basketball or soccer. Or, turn on the radio and have a dance-off!

STAY SAFE

✔ **Protect** your bones! Wear a helmet, knee pads, elbow pads, and wrist guards when skating or skateboarding. And wear proper gear when playing sports such as hockey or football.

BODY BOOST

✔ Your bones need a mineral called calcium to be strong. Dairy products such as milk, yogurt, and cheese contain calcium. So do green vegetables!

✔ Vitamin D is good for your bones. You can get vitamin D from being in the sun. It is also in milk and some yogurts and cereals.

Important Words

blood vessel a tube that carries blood throughout the body.

flexible able to bend or move easily.

mineral a natural substance. Minerals make up rocks and other parts of nature.

muscles (MUH-suhls) body tissues, or layers of cells, that help move the body.

organ a body part that does a special job. The heart and the lungs are organs.

protect (pruh-TEHKT) to guard against harm or danger.

spinal cord a cord of nerves inside the spine that carries messages between your brain and your body.

tissue (TIH-shoo) a group of cells that form a part of a living thing.

Web Sites

To learn more about the skeletal system, visit ABDO Publishing Company online. Web sites about the skeletal system are featured on our Book Links page. These links are routinely monitored and updated to provide the most current information available.

www.abdopublishing.com

Index